Goethe's Divan for Divination

Compiled and edited
By Chris Gibson

About

Goethe's Divan for Divination originally started life as an artist's book made for an exhibition called *Poieses* at ArtSpace Dusseldorf. For this group show artists were invited to create an artwork inspired by an existing text.

I learned that Goethe's *Divan* was written as an homage to the 14th century poet Hafez, whose own *Divan* has been used through the centuries for bibliomancy (fortune-telling by picking a poem at random). The colourful and romantic nature of Goethe's poetry, also made it ideal for divination.

I love the idea that consulting a book with an idea or theme in mind, might reveal insight or direction, as if someone else's words and ideas can act like a mirror and allow us to see ourselves or our situations differently. For ease of access, this book is split into six chapters, each with six poems. If you are looking for inspiration, the poems can be dipped into at random, either by using dice, or picking a theme.

As an artist I've been working with books, text and language for many years. For me books are intimate and personal objects which can be experienced differently by each person who reads them. I hope you enjoy this book and dipping in and out of Goethe's poems.

Chris Gibson

Methods of Divination

With Dice

With a question in mind roll two dice. With the first select a chapter and with the second a poem. Read the poem once, letting the words wash over you. Visualise the imagery in the text. Read again with your question in mind to look for guidance.

By Theme

Theme	Poem	Theme	Poem
Adventure	1.1	Discovery	1.2
Attraction	5.4	Divinity	6.4
Beauty	5.3	Dogmatism	6.3
Beguilement	3.2	Dreams	5.1
Belief	2.1	Enchantment	6.4
Birth	5.2	Enlightenment	2.5
Brightness	1.3	Entrapment	3.2
Candidness	4.6	Envy	3.6
Changeability	5.6	Escape	1.1
Charm	5.3	Eternity	3.1
Civility	4.1	Faith	2.1
Comfort	5.5	Family	6.2
Commitment	3.6	Fantasy	3.5
Compassion	4.1	Foresight	5.1
Concealment	2.6	Freedom	1.2
Confusion	1.4	Grief	3.4
Continuation	6.6	Growth	5.2
Controversy	2.2	Happiness	4.4
Creation	1.5	Harmony	1.6
Desire	5.4	Heartbreak	3.1

Themes Continued

Theme	Poem	Theme	Poem
Honour	6.3	Reason	2.2
Humanity	5.2	Rebellion	2.3
Humility	6.5	Relationships	3.6
Idealism	5.3	Religion	2.1
Imagination	3.5	Respect	4.2
Infatuation	3.5	Revelation	1.2
Insight	2.5	Reverence	4.2
Inspiration	1.5	Reward	6.1
Joy	1.3	Righteousness	6.3
Kinship	2.4	Safety	6.5
Knowledge	2.5	Satisfaction	4.4
Lightness	1.3	Searching	1.6
Limit	4.5	Sickness	5.5
Lineage	6.2	Simplicity	4.6
Longing	6.4	Slavery	5.4
Lover	3.3	Solitude	5.6
Lovers	3.1	Sorrow	3.4
Melancholy	5.6	Stability	4.3
Paradise	6.6	Strength	2.3
Passion	3.3	Support	5.5
Perfection	1.5	Time	4.5
Plainness	4.6	Transformation	4.3
Poetry	2.4	Transgression	2.3
Potency	2.6	Transience	4.5
Potential	5.1	Truth	2.2
Preference	6.5	Virtue	4.1
Prize	6.1	Wandering	1.4
Promise	6.1	Wealth	4.4
Rapture	3.3	Worship	4.2

ONE
~

Book of the Singer
Moghanni Nameh

1.1
Sense of Freedom

Let me exulting in my saddle ride!
While in your tents and huts ye may abide;
And joyfully I'll ride afar,
Naught o'er my turban but the star.*

The stars as guides on land and seas
He places in the sky,
That ye yourselves with them may please
Whene'er ye look on high.†

---

* Based on the answer of a Caucasian Chief, who, when submission was proposed to him, said he could see nothing above him but heaven.
† Founded on a verse in the Quran.

1.2
Confession

The monster fire is hard to conceal,[*]
For smoke will show its place by day;
By night its flame will all reveal.
Nor love can one easier hide away;
However closely you may confine,
From sparkling eyes it is sure to shine.
A poem's the hardest of all to hide,
For under a bushel 'twill not abide.
For should it the poet have newly made,
His very being it must pervade,
And when he has written it neat and fair,
The whole of the world must for it care;
Whether it please or whether it bore,
He reads it to ev'ry one more and more.

---

[*] Based on a saying of Agricola: "Four things cannot be hidden: Fire, for where fire is there is smoke and steam or heat: then a cough, an eruption, and lastly love, which is blind, and fancies no one can see it."

1.3
Phenomenon

Let with the wall of rain
Phoebus unite,—
Quick shines the bow again
In coloured light.

Drawn in the cloud I see
Twin arc of light,—
Still bow of heav'n 'twill be,
Though it be white.

Let not, then, joyous sage,
Sorrow thee move:
White though thy hair with age,
Yet wilt thou love.*

---

* The appearance of a rainbow with a faint, colourless reflection, the twin arc, seems to have given the poet occasion to think of himself in his old age as still capable of love.

1.4
Distraction

By the brook on the left
Cupid's flute playing;
In the field on the right
Mars' trumpet braying.
Thither the list'ning ear
Lovingly bends,
Misled by false alarm
Where the song wends.
Still sounds the flute so glad
'Midst war's loud thunder:
I become raving, mad,
Is that a wonder?
Still does the flute resound,
Still trumpet brays:
Raving, I wander round:
Why in amaze?*

---

* Hafez says:
"Bring wine, of heav'n's deceit one never can be sure
Whilst Venus harping and her champion Mars allure."
   This piece is a very difficult one to translate so as to keep the original metre and yet give a general idea of the poet's meaning, the distraction of his mind between the allurements of war and peace. A literal translation is quite unattainable.

1.5
Song and Statuary

With the forms he makes of clay
Let the Greek exhaust his art,
With the son of his own hands
Swell the rapture of his heart.

Yet to us a source of joy
With Euphrates' stream to play,
In its limpid element,
Hither now, now thither sway.

Quench I so the soul's bright brand,
Song will ever loud resound;
Dipped by poet's cleanly hand
Water will preserve its round.*

---

* There is a Hindu tradition, made use of in another of Goethe's poems, that water can be taken up like a ball in the hand of a pure woman. The general scope of this piece seems to be that he who has enjoyed the perfection of Greek statuary should also refresh himself with the flowing forms of Eastern poetry, which he will attain to if he first calms down his own soul, as water can be taken up in the hand of a pure woman.

1.6
Self-Confidence

In what is all the secret found
That man should healthy be?
Each should delight to hear the sound
That tends to harmony.

Away with what disturbs thy course!
Away with gloomy strife!
Before he sings, or ceases song,
The poet must have life.

Then though the brazen clang of life
May through the spirit roar!
Poets will reconcile themselves
Though they at heart be sore.

TWO
~

Book of Hafez
Hafez Nameh

2.1
Poet

Hafez, then it seems to me
I need not give way to thee;
For when we think as others do,
Become we like those others, too,
And thus I quite resemble thee,
For from our holy Books in me
A glorious form assumed you see.
(As on that cloth of cloths impressed
The image of our Lord did rest.)[*]
Thus to my tranquil soul relief,
Though robbed, denied, and with restraint oppressed,
Came in the glad form of belief.[†]

---

[*] This refers to the legend of St. Veronica.
[†] Goethe says of himself with regard to his knowledge of the Bible:
"For almost alone to it do I owe my moral culture, and the events, the teachings, the symbols, the similes of it, had impressed themselves deeply I upon me, and operated on me in one way or another." He allowed in Hafez not only a thorough knowledge of the Quran, but also a pious I practice of its precepts. He was a religious teacher in Shirâz. The last line but one was aimed against Voltaire's infidelity and mockery of Christianity.

2.2
Judgment

All thy poetic fancies, Hafez, show
The light of inextinguishable truth,
But here and there, too, there are little things
That lie beyond the boundary of law.
Wouldst thou proceed in safety, thou shouldst know
Snake's venom to resolve from antidote.
It surely were the best, so not to err,
To the pure luxury oneself to give
Of noble action with a courage high,
And from all such as bring but ceaseless pain
Oneself to guard with a well-reasoned mind.
This the poor Ebussuud* indites to you.
(May God have grace and pardon all his sins!)

---

* Ebussuud Efendi was a celebrated Mufti, or Judge, in the time of Suleiman I, at Constantinople. The judgment, in the case of Hafez's poems, is that, although they contain many undeniable truths, yet here and there there are in them little things that are beyond the boundary of the law, i.e. unlawful. The best plan, therefore, is to distinguish between them as one distinguishes snake-poison from its antidote, to follow what is good, and avoid what may draw in its train only eternal pain.

2.3
The German Renders Thanks

O holy Ebussuud, exactly so!
It is such saints the poet wishes for,
For 'tis precisely in those little things
That he beyond the limits of the law
That lies the patrimony where he, proud,
Excites himself with pleasure in his grief.
Snake's venom and its antidote to him
The one just like the other must appear;
One will not kill, the other will not cure.
For perfect life is ever in one's acts
To deal with innocence, which proves itself
In doing wrong to no one but itself.
So may the ancient poet have a hope
In Paradise above that Houris* fair
As a transfigured youth may him receive.
O holy Ebussuud, exactly so!

---

* Houris. The enchanting heavenly maids appointed to wait on the True Believers in the Muslim Paradise. They figure elsewhere in the "Divan."

2.4
To Hafez

Hafez, if I with thee compare,
What folly 'twere!
Swiftly and proud upon the tide
Though bark may ride,
Bold and proud wandering, its sail
Swell with the gale,—
Yet should the sea in splinters tear,
'Twould float, rotten there.
In light and sprightly melody
The cool flood sways for thee,
But boiling over, with its fiery fume
Will me consume.
A thought will yet rise in my heart
And strength impart,
I've lived in lands of sunny hue,
And I have loved there, too.*

---

* Commentators differ as to whether the sunny land referred to is Italy, where he had been so happy, or the figurative land of his love. The simile of the shipwreck is adopted by Hafez, in imitation of whose style the piece is composed. The Berlin edition remarks: "To rival Hafez was a dangerous undertaking, on which the poet would only venture in remembrance of the sunny days of love which he had once lived through."

2.5
Open Secret

O holy and reverend Hafez,
They call thee the mystical tongue,[*]
But who of the words knows the purport
There's no one the learned among.

With them thou art truly a mystic;
They think all is folly that's thine,
And thus in thy name without reason
Retail their unsavoury wine.

Because they can not understand thee,
To them a pure mystic art thou,
Who, though not devout, art yet blessed!
Though this they will never allow.

---

[*] Hafez was called the mystical tongue (Lisan ool ghaib), because his words had superhuman power and mysterious purport. In order not to condemn Hafez, the True Believers endeavour to make out that his sensual love was merely an allegory of that which is godlike, and his drunkenness an image of heavenly ecstasy.

2.6
Sign*

Yet those I blame may still be in the right,
A simple word itself can have no might
To all must be self-evident, indeed.
A word is but a fan! Between the sticks
On thee a pretty pair of eyes themselves can fix.
The fan resembles but a lovely mead,
For though the face from me it truly hide,
The maid herself concealed may not abide;
For what is fairest in her beauty bright,
Her eye, still flashes on me with its light.

---

* A word has not an existence of its own, but is only a sign or indication of what is understood by it. Saadi likens words to a veil over the face of a pretty woman, or the moon behind a cloud, and Goethe here likens them to a fan held by a girl, whose sparkling eyes shine out between the sticks. The piece is a humorous hit at the interpreters of mysticism. Saadi says: "Each of my rules in this book is a cover, spread before the face of a fair woman; under each letter is hidden an interpretation, as a fair picture hides itself under a screen and the moon under clouds."

THREE

~

Book of Love
Ishk Nameh

3.1
Another Pair[*]

Yes, loving always is great pain:
Who may find fairer in the main?
Not power nor wealth will it provide,
But places thee by heroes' side.
For of the Prophet he who tales can tell
Of Wâmik and of Asra speaks as well.
One need not talk, one only has to name,
They are so wide and fully known to fame.
What they have done, or how they moved
That no man knows: but that they loved
We know full well. To answer easy task
When men of Wâmik and of Asra ask.

---

[*] Nothing is known of Wâmik and Asra but that they loved each other, and their loves are famous.

3.2
Warned*

To curling locks have I myself
Too willing captive made;
So, Hafez, to thy friend as thee
The same trick has been played.

But their tresses now they weave
Out of the longest hair;
Under this morion they fight,
As we can all declare.

But he who due precaution takes
Will not be caught again:
He runs into the lightest noose,
But fears a heavy chain.

---

* Imitated from Hafez:
"My heart has entangled itself in the net of thy looks,"
and aimed at a particular style of coiffure adopted by the ladies of the day.

3.3
Absorbed

Curl full of curls that little head so round!
With both hands full, in such rich, streaming hair,
Might I to wander up and down but dare,
Then from my heart myself might I feel sound.
And when I kiss that mouth, those eyes, that brow,
I am refreshed, though wounded just as now.
The five-tongued comb,* where shall I place it, where?
Again it nestles in those tresses fair.
A soft caress denies me not the ear,
I feel no flesh, and there is no skin here,
So tender to be toyed with, full of love!
And as around that little head we move,
Oh! would that in those flowing tresses still
One could for ever wander up and down at will!
Thou, Hafez, also hast the same thing done:
For long ago we both have this begun.

---

* By the five tongued comb is signified the hand, which nestles in the beloved one's hair.

3.4
Poor Consolation[*]

At midnight I both wept and sobbed,
For I was far from thee.
Then came the spirits of night,
And I was ashamed.
"Spirits of night," I said;
"Weeping and sobbing:
Now do ye find me, whom once
Ye had pass'd by as I slept.
Many good things I have lost.
Think not the worse of me,
Who once ye thought was so wise:
Great misfortune has happened."
Then the spirits of night
With longest of faces
Passed them along,
If I wise were or foolish
Quite unconcerned.

---

* Founded on Hafez:
"At all the blood, that yesternight
Flowed from the storehouse of my eyes,
Before the ghosts of dreams I sit
Ashamed, that weird at night arise."
Also:
"The night of parting threw a shade:
What games the ghosts of fancy played!"

3.5
Inevitable

Who can command in the meadow
Silence the birds to keep?*
And who can forbid at the shearing
To struggle the bleating sheep?

Am I, then, becoming unruly
When crispily curls my wool?
No! the shearer cures my impatience,
As my hair he does worry and pull.

Who will prevent me from singing,
As I list to the heavens above,
To the clouds above me intrusting
How she has bewitched me with love?†

---

* Imitated from Hafez:
"Can one, then, not whisper, 'Hush'
To the bird that's in the bush?"
The simile of the sheep is Goethe's own.

† Explained by Düntzer to be the expression of the repressed condition of the lover, who must give out in some way the feelings of his love and longing, and who can no more be forced to silence than a bird in the bush, or to be still more than a sheep being shorn. If in no other way, he must express his feelings to the clouds.

3.6
Secret

At my pretty sweetheart's ogling.*
Look the people in surprise:
I, the knowing one, on my part
Know full well what it implies.

It means this: I love but this man,
And I love none else beside:
So may all of ye, good people,
Curious longings lay aside.

Yes: with very fierce expression
At the crowd her glances lour,
But she only tries to tell me
Of the next delightful hour.

---

* Düntzer mistranslates Hafez, with reference to this. It is really as follows:
"Wonder all the inexperienced
At the ogling of my eyes (not those of the beloved);
I am only what I've shown them,
Though they think me otherwise."

FOUR
~

Book of Reflections
Tufkîr Nameh

4.1
Five Things[*]

Five things with five are never fraught:
Open thy ear wide and be taught,
From haughty breast will never friendship grow.
Politeness seek not in companions low:
A scampish fellow never can to greatness rise:
The naked finds no pity in a miser's eyes:
For faith and confidence the liar hopes in vain,
Of these let none deprive thee, but for aye maintain.

---

[*] Imitated from the Book of Counsel of Farid ud-Din Attar, a Persian poet.

4.2
To Shah Shuja and Others like Him*

Above the Transoxanian throng,
Shouting in thy praise,
Upon thy road our song
Heartily we raise.
In thy rule secure
All our life is past.
May thy life endure!
May thy kingdom last.†

---

* The Duke of Weimar under the name of Shah Shuja; this was Jalal ud-Din, the fourth of the Mozaffari dynasty, under whom Hafez lived, and wrote much in his honour. The martial music of the countries beyond the Oxus was celebrated.
† Hafez says:
"If to the world thou wishest good,
Ask for a long life for the king."

4.3
The Highest Favour*

Untamed as once I used to be,
I have now a master found:
Tamed but after many years,
I a mistress, too, have found.
As they trial did not spare,
True and faithful I was found,
Nursed and kept with ev'ry care
As a treasure they had found.
None two masters can obey,
Or therein has fortune found,
Master, mistress, gladly see
That they both of them me found.
Fortune's star is bright as day,
Since I both of them have found.

Through many lands have I travelling been,
And everywhere crowds of people have seen;
In every corner have searched right well:
On every blade for me grain would swell.
Such blessed towns have I never espied,
With Huris on Huris, and bride upon bride.

---

* The form of this piece is a close imitation of the Persian style. Written as an expression of esteem towards the Duke and Duchess of Weimar, the latter of whom at first disliked Goethe, but afterwards came round to trusting him entirely.

4.4
Firdusi[*] Speaks

O world, how shameless and wicked art thou!
Thou rearest and cheerest and killest as well.
He only from Allah who favour receives,
Lively and rich, self-sustaining, will dwell.

What, then, are riches? A life-giving sun,[†]
The beggar enjoys it, as we, too, have done,
And let not the rich his love ever take ill,
That love that is happy in stubborn self-will.

---

[*] Firdusi, author of the Shahnameh, maintained of himself that he could have said much better all that Muhammad had said.
[†] Riches consist in enjoyment, so the beggar that enjoys himself stubbornly in the sunshine, without being moved out of it by any one, enjoys great riches, and should not be found fault with by the rich.

4.5
Jalal ad-Din Rumi Speaks*

If in the world thou lingerest, as dream it flies apace,
And if thou movest onwards, fate restricts the space.
Nor heat nor cold art thou enabled fast to hold,
And that which blooms for thee is also growing old.

---

* In answer to this warning by Jalal ad-Din, that this world and all that are in it are fleeting, Zuleika is supposed to point out that God is eternal, and her beauty is a reflection from Him.

4.6
Zuleika Speaks

That I am fair my mirror makes me understand!
Ye say that to grow old my fate must also be.
All in God's presence must for ever stand;
Love for a moment, therefore, Him in loving me.

FIVE
~

Book of Zuleika
Zuleika Nameh

5.1
Zuleika

As I on Euphrates sailed,
Stripped itself off in the sea,
That gold ring from off my finger
Which thou lately gavest me.

Thus I dreamt. Then through the trees
Dazed my eye morn's rosy beam.
Tell me, poet! tell me, prophet!
What signifies to me the dream?

5.2
Gingo Biloba

This tree's leaves from Eastern regions
To my garden that are brought,
To the knowing with a flavour
Of a secret sense are fraught:

Is it, then, a living being,
Splitting, that divided grew?
Are they two that chose each other,
So that both as one we knew?

Such deep questioning to answer
The right fancy I can see.
Feel'st thou not from all my ditties,
I can one and double be?*

---

* The leaves of this tree divide themselves at the point into two. Its botanical name is the Salisburia Adiantifolia.

5.3
Hâtem

Yes, with sweet yet mighty glances,
Smile that every heart entrances—
And with teeth so dazzling clear*
Eye-lash dart,† snake locks that neck
And bosom fair surrounding deck,
Things a thousand-fold to fear.
Now reflect how from of old
Fair Zuleika was foretold.

---

* A frequent simile with Hafez.
† Imitated from Hafez:
"Strike not my heart with the darts on thy eye-lids."

5.4
Maidens

A poet's such a willing slave,—
Rule, he thinks, from service springs,
Yet above all should it please him
If herself his loved one sings.

Is she capable of songs,
As upon our lips they play?
For it mates her much suspected
That she holds such secret sway.

5.5
The Loving One speaks

Why does the Captain
Not send his messenger,
Not send him daily
Here to my comfort?
Sure he has horses,
Knows how to write, too.

He can write Tâlik,
Neski he knows, too:
Sweetly he writes it
On silken pages.
In place of himself, then,
He should aye write me.

Can not the sick one,
Will not recover
From her sweet sorrow.
She at the tidings
From her beloved one
Sickens, though healthy.

5.6
Echo

It sounds so grandly when a poet
In sun or emperor his likeness takes,
Yet as in dusky night he slinks away,
He hides the mournful faces that he makes.

By clouds encompassed in their heavy folds,
Sank down to night the purest Hue of day;
My cheeks emaciated are so pale,
And my heart's tears become a leaden grey.

My best beloved, of the moon-like face,
Oh! leave me not to pain and to the night;
My lamp, my phosphorus art thou,
My sun art thou, and thou art too, my light!

SIX
~

Book of Paradise
Khoold Nameh

6.1
Foretaste

The True Believer speaks of Paradise,
As if himself he always there had been:
The promises of the Quran he trusts,
Thus taught, upon its precepts he will lean.

And yet the Prophet, author of the Book,
Can there above appreciate our need,
And sees, despite the thunder of his curse,
How Faith's embittered by the doubts we plead.

Thus he sends down from the eternal spheres
Youth's model* all to render young again:
Swaying she floats her down, and on my neck
Of lovely ringlets clasps around the chain.

To bosom and to heart so close I press
The heav'nly thing; I need no farther wiss:
I have no farther doubt of Paradise,
For ever trustingly I her would kiss.

---

* The model of youth, promised in the Quran, that floats down from above, is one of the Houris.

6.2
Chosen Women

None of these joys should women lose,
In all sincerity to hope we dare,
And still of womankind as yet we know,
Of only four who were admitted there.

First Zuleika, earthly sun,
Who tow'rds Joseph was inflamed,
Love of Paradise now won,
Of resignation gem is famed.

Then comes she, who ever-blessed,
Grieving for her bitter loss,
Bearing heathens' safety, cheated,
Saw her son lost on the cross.

His weal and glory who built up,
Next she who was Muhammad's wife,
Who one to trust in and one God,
Recommended in her life.

And then comes Fatimah, the fair,
Daughter and faultless consort, there,
Purest soul of angels' mould,
In a form of honey gold.

These are the four that there we find.
And he who sings a woman's praise,
In everlasting homes with these,
Deserves to roam to endless days.*

---

* Zuleika was Potiphar's wife. She, Mary the mother of Christ, Muhammad's wife (the third wife, Aisha), and Fatimah his daughter, the four mentioned here as the chosen women, differ from the four to whom the Muslims assign places in Paradise. They were Ahia, Pharaoh's wife, Mirza, Amran's daughter, Khadeiza, Muhammad's wife, and Fatimah, his daughter. The Quran says that Christ was taken up alive into heaven,

6.3
Houri

To-day I stand upon my watch
Outside the gates of Paradise:
I know not what I ought to do,
Thou art in such suspicious guise.

To our Brothers of the Faith
Art thou strict and truly kin,
That thy battles and thy merits
To Paradise should let thee in?

Count'st thou thyself among those heroes?
What thy wounds are do thou show,
That proclaim to me thy honour,
That I may let thee onwards go.

Goethe's account being the accepted Christian version. The piece concludes with the promise that all poets who have sung in praise of women as he has will enjoy Paradise in their company. There is a second version of this in Hempel's edition, which is not inserted here.

6.4
Poet

Thy love, thy kiss, enchant me still!
Into thy secrets I would never pry,
Yet tell me if, descending from the sky,
Thou hast not had a mortal birth?
To me the thought is often borne,
I almost think I might be sworn,
Zuleika thou wast named on earth.

6.5
The Favoured Beasts

Four animals were bidden
To Paradise to come:
There with pious, holy men,
Is their eternal home.

The preference had the donkey here,—
He came with steps so gay,
For Jesus to the prophets' town
Upon him rode one day.

Commended to Muhammad comes
The wolf half timid there:
"Now, leave the poor man there his sheep:
For the rich go seek elsewhere."

With wagging tail, so gay and true,
The dog his faith that kept
To his own lord when in the cave,
The seven together slept.

Abu Hurairah's cat its lord
Purrs round, for ever blessed,
For that must be a holy beast
The Prophet has caressed.*

---

* According to Oriental tradition there will be admitted into Paradise Abraham's ram, the ant and Solomon's hoopoe, the prophet Jeremiah or Ezra's ass, Jonah's whale, the oxen of Moses, Noah's dove, Muhammad's Burak or Camel, and St. George's horse. The dog of the seven sleepers was allowed in also with them. Muhammad is said to have pointed out a better prey to the wolf than the hind it had caught. This appears to be the only reason why it has been admitted among the four by Goethe. Abu Hurairah in Arabic means the father of cats: one of Muhammad's friends was so called, because he was always accompanied by a cat.

6.6
Good-night

Now, loved songs, be laid to rest
Of my people on the breast.
In musk-scented cloud of sleep
Gabriel the members keep
Of this weary one at length!
That he, fresh with youthful strength,
Gay, convivial as ever,
May the rock's dark fissures sever;
So with heroes of all days
He may walk in pleasure's ways,
Where the fair, the ever-new,
From all sides may itself renew,
And on Paradise's plain
Infinity rejoice again;
Yes, the dog, the faithful, true,
Accompany his masters, too.*

---

* Written by Goethe as a wind-up to the Divan. He dedicates the songs to his people, the Germans; but desires that Gabriel may shut him himself up in a rocky cave, as the seven sleepers and the dog were and translate him to Paradise in like manner with them.

ISBN: 978-0-9957728-4-7

Front Cover Images:
Night Sky by Luck Galindo
Goethe etching by Johann Heinrich Lips
Atlas bearing the heavens by William Cunningham

Back Cover Image:
Detail from doublures inside a Divan of Hafez, 1842

www.chrisgibsonart.com